Change the Way You Face the Day

ALSO BY ALLAN COX

WHOA! Are They Glad You're in their Lives?

The CEO in You

Your Inner CEO

Redefining Corporate Soul (with Julie Liesse)

Straight Talk for Monday Morning

The Achiever's Profile

The Making of the Achiever

Inside Corporate America

Work, Love and Friendship

Confessions of a Corporate Headhunter

Change the Way You Face the Day

By

Allan Cox

Harrier Press™

Harrier Press™

Published by
Harrier Press
Chicago, Illinois 60611
U.S.A.
www.HarrierPress.com

Manufactured in the United States of America
10 9 8 7 6 5 4 3 2
First Edition 2013

Library of Congress Cataloging-in Publication Data

Cox, Allan, 1937–
Change the Way You Face the Day / Allan Cox
p. cm.
ISBN 978-1-938610-06-6
1. Poetry.   2. Thought and thinking.   3. Leadership.   4. Self-Growth.
5. Inspiration.   I. Title.

Designed by Big B Consulting, LLC

For Brack, the man, my dad

They are watershed moments. At such intervals, the whole life is seen as a single entity of time. There is the special role of the moment that becomes the moment—a current of energy, power, illumination—there are many names for it. But life takes on a "whiff" of density—a moment of raw sanction given to the very idiom of the life itself.

—Howard Thurman

[CONTENTS]

What Do I Do Now?

TRAMPLED

Are you on the road
to stop?
I mean, how long
will you travel?
Do you wonder
how much
you should endure?
You look tired
friend,
like someone
worn out from
washing clean clothes.
Are you needed
elsewhere,
the you you've
trampled under
your own feet?
Shatter them!
They're only clay.
Roll yourself
in a cart
to that river
alongside
and meet there
your invisible
angel
and feet of
wings.

Sometimes old convictions make us old before our time.

What questions, if any, have you entertained lately that raise doubts about your life course?

Should you choose to change course, how bold can you be without having the new path laid out clearly?

Where will you find support if you change course? It's there to be found.

What still, small voice has kept you alive amid doubt and confusion?

What lights you up? Think back to some good times for clues. Go to the light.

Watch your feet. Where are they taking you?

See How We Look Up

ICON

Over the man's chair,
where he finds comfort
with his books
hangs a print
of an angel made
of carved wood—
a statue that in
its real life
stands 12 feet tall.
He's playing his pipe
in praise—that angel—
as memorialized in
the 150th Psalm.
The man in the chair
sees less of him
than you might think,
as the angel remains
at his back.
Perhaps that's the point—
acknowledged by his
furtive bow as he
enters the room.

We all benefit from looking up.

One of architecture's great inventions is the arch.

The man knows the real angel and that's why he bought the print, framed it, and placed it above his head. He's seen the angel, he is real.

Do you have a nook where your comfort is safe? Where your mind is quieted?

We seat ourselves, lean back, look up and feel at ease, sigh (even) maybe. Then we look down, don't we? Is this true for you?

We are made for worship.

We each have our angel, who is not meant to be denied.

Visions in the Backyard

BLADE

I'm leaning sunward slightly,
    just doing my job, one of a
    million billion blades of grass,
    maybe more, in the backyard
    of this family. I'm not standing

tall as I was yesterday because the
    dad mowed the lawn, as he put it,
    and lopped off my top. This afternoon,
    though, the young boy in the house is
    stretched out on his stomach on us,

looking at our numbers intently. He's
    gliding his palm softly over our chopped
    tops. Oh, now he's pushed back a clump
    of us and seems to be taking a special
    interest in me. He grabs me between his

thumb and forefinger and yanks me out from my
    root. He places my white base into his mouth,
    sucks on it, rolls it around his tongue; tastes
    something sweet about me. He rolls over
    on his back, closes his eyes,

basks in the warm sun, and keeps my company.
    Then his mother calls him in. He stands,
    lifts me out of his mouth, flips me to the
    ground, and then goes in. In a couple of
    days, I'll be dried and withered and

go my way. No matter. I've done my job. I ask, not idly,
    would you like to know my supreme joy, having
    reached my full stature, and stood proudly in
    many suns? Merely this: Having been seen—
    really seen—by this sweet boy.

Empathy, they say, soothes our hurts.

Have you ever thought about the life of a blade of grass? The rose gets much attention, but what of the ordinary grass that grows? Does it not have a stem just like the rose?

What of the lawnmower blade that cuts the blades?

Were it to breathe, it would merely sigh at the question.

How do you feel when you're seen for who you are?

It's obvious you are visible, but are you seen?

And yes, I must ask, are you seeable?

When Life is Living in the Fold

Her

How does he know her,
    that executive with eyes that shine,
        and a giver's pulse,
            with forgiveness in hand,
                and . . . so quickly hurt?

but for her glance that holds,
    the quick embrace,
        her heart-born touch,
            and . . . doubt a whisk.

but for her electrified hurl,
    a toter's arm and leg,
        her sure reach for what makes do,
            and . . . harshness that scuttles.

but for making good's case,
    hearing none but compassion's voice,
        lighting up those drawn to her,
            and . . . a will for worry.

but as mirror to his faults,
    and gifts as well,
        a link—a bond, even—to those he cherishes,
            and . . . impatience that snuffs.

More, still, does he know her
    as a pilgrim, yes,
    believer in him and the powers,
    soul to him in love without words,
    and her the creator, hearth and home.

Love with her?
    Look at him see her right now, taking a nap, tiny triangle
    of her face covered by the crumpled sheet, eyes, nose, lips,
    serene, peeking pretty. If he ever walked out the door, he
    wouldn't make it past the first step.

The greatest gift in the world of love is the love of someone, not from someone.

To be blown away permanently by a partner—ever and always—is psychic perpetual motion.

To love fully is to be snapped to attention.

When anger comes, as it will, it cannot, does not, have the heart to last.

We ask men to find their feminine side, but women can, at least in apparel, find their masculine side with ease.

Being in love is to know you'll never be alone, knowing how not to be alone.

Yet love makes solitude rich.

Life in Firefly Village

CURB

We, boys mostly,
sat on the curb
in our town
wherever we
met to play
ball in the streets.
Sometimes we sat
there with a
portable radio, listening
to some game that mattered.
The curb was
the starting place,
the spectator place,
the ending place,
when our time
in the street
was done,
when we might hear
someone's mother call
her son to lunch or supper.
There were times,
too, after supper
when our dads would
join us, till it
began to get dark
and we'd sit on the curb,
laugh and tell stories,
and watch the fireflies.

It is intriguing how community takes place and people adhere to form and structure.

I had a professor, a sociologist, who defined socialization as the process whereby a biological blob becomes a social slob.

It is amazing, too, how simple good will get things started in a positive way.

Perhaps you can't go home again, but you can savor what home gave you.

It was a slower time but life still requires we make the most of the fallow time, when more happens than what we see.

Me? I like to watch tall grass bend in the wind.

Have you seen any fireflies lately?

That Thing Is Life in the Wings!

It

"How will you
do it?"
she asked.
He didn't know
and said so.
It depends
on the it,
he said.
Since hearing
that exchange,
I've wondered
about *my* it,
there,
waiting.

If you've announced something, people want to see how you do. It's true, isn't it?

It's not that they love you, necessarily; they want to see if you can deliver.

People's motives vary and are their own. It's best not to take your bows, even when you succeed. That makes your mark more strongly.

The more significant question is what is your It? That's your heavy homework.

What is It, really, you need to do and not look the other way?

What has intruded in your thought process lately, that has you thinking about It? That's your own hound of heaven.

Make sure the It is under your skin. This is the only way to live!

The Way It Is

Work

The ways of work
the ways of people
to get things done
to get things done right
to get right things done right.
What about getting the
wrong things done right?
Doesn't it work out
sometimes to end up
at the wrong address?
You might meet something
or somebody you're
supposed to . . .
Tolerance, tolerance,
is what I say!
Let's find some blessedness
in mistakes.
Yes, let's laugh
right now.
It was supposed
to be
this
way.

Life is just flat out wondrous.

Think how nice and free-form not
to be in control. Wrap your arms
around those times. Roll with them.

Think how often we would have
screwed up if we had done it our way.

Of course, we do get it right most
of the time, when our competence
shines and we're true to the call.

So flexibility is key, with an openness
to see how things are in the moment.

Markets surprise us; stun us might
be a better way to put it. Who would
think our product or service could
have met that need?

Let's lighten up and enjoy being
startled. We've been blessed.

When the Seemingly Insignificant Isn't

PHOTO

That photo, nothing
special, sits idly
in a collection
over there
on the dresser,
often not seen,
and seen past.
Yet some mornings,
it's one of the first
things I take in—clearly,
forcefully, in its soft
warm leather frame,
wearing well and
asserting itself
appropriately.
The phone rings;
out the window,
a day gray as wool,
a call that matters to me.
As I stand and talk
and turn, looking,
the photo
looks back at me,
and I remember.

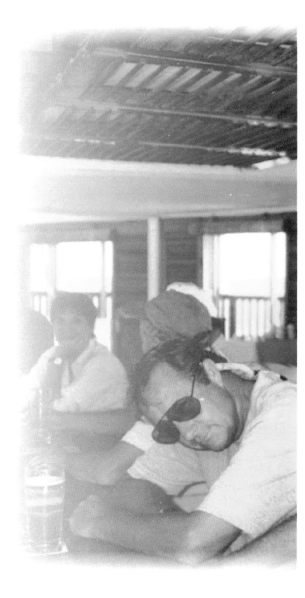

The seasonality of a happening may not conform to any calendar.

Nor is it necessarily of the same length or intensity when it repeats.

Such it is with a photo in our bedroom that has its special moment—not just once but periodically.

Look at the photo. The three of us, along with our wives, have just completed a five-day safari in Kenya.

We're in a lodge bar, waiting to be taken to a small airport from which we'll fly two hours away to the Seychelles Islands.

I'm the one standing. This was 15 years ago or more. I had just told a joke that made *mis amigos* groan.

A bond formed. It is something special which makes life better, never to be forgotten. It's how things can be.

See What Isn't There,
Then Put It There

Leaf

Sitting still
in the corner chair
just past dawn
listening—the window
wide open—
buoyant on the birds' frolics.
One flew in, pecked me
on my left earlobe
and whispered
"Come with me."
I did and she propped me
up on a dew-dropped leaf
to spritely waves
on the morning's breeze,
whereupon I spent the day.
And, when I returned home,
was surprised to hear
my love's sweet query:
your journey . . . tell me,
how was it?

Creating and entertaining fantasies is one of the best ways I know to acknowledge what I want!

It's a mistake not to know what you want. Some truly may not know and others are embarrassed to say. Wake up. Don't be embarrassed.

Suppose you saw The Horse Whisperer starring Robert Redford, and found out you love horses. In a way, you never knew what you wanted.

So how do you imagine yourself in a life with a horse even if you've seldom or never have been near one?

Let it fly. Ride one like the wind or nurture a sick one back to life—all in your mind.

Own the feeling. After all, this is you, what you care about. It's your creation, bubbled up within. You can't fake or deny that!

Make your plan. Write an email. Place your phone call. Get in touch with somebody to take the next step. Get to know a horse!

It Comes in on Little Cat Feet

Turning

She was
ruminating
among us.
It bore its way
softly—
as a breaking dawn—
to our small band
and to her
that she hadn't meant
to do this,
to declare her treasures
and share her travels
so quietly, forcefully.
The keepsakes for us
were the incidentals
of how she came
to be here,
how the events
unfolded—
led to our
little assembly
and why she
believed we
belonged together
in the undertaking—
our agenda withered,
our real work,
begun.

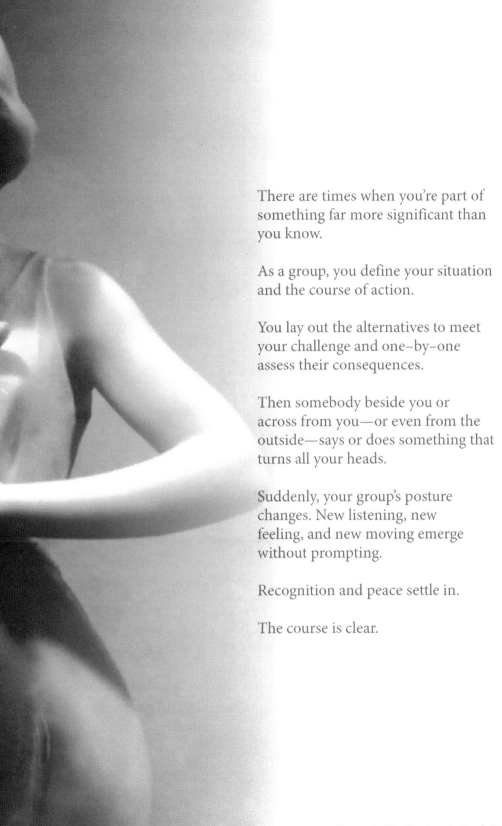

There are times when you're part of something far more significant than you know.

As a group, you define your situation and the course of action.

You lay out the alternatives to meet your challenge and one–by–one assess their consequences.

Then somebody beside you or across from you—or even from the outside—says or does something that turns all your heads.

Suddenly, your group's posture changes. New listening, new feeling, and new moving emerge without prompting.

Recognition and peace settle in.

The course is clear.

Be Present at the Creation

THERE

It's one thing
to have a curiosity
and satisfy it—
say, how massive
construction machinery
gets built.
What, though, to make
of bolts from the blue?
A long absent friend appears
in your thoughts
and one day soon,
on the street before you.
A piece of work—
that fits your gifts—
leaps forward
from a phone call.
A last minute idea
wriggles free
at the moment
of delivery,
sprinkling fairy dust.
A casual question you raise
opens a new world.

    So, truth told,
    you've been there . . .
    what do you
    make of it,
    really,

    this time?

As school-aged children we could say, with wide eyes and much delight, of events that were stranger than fiction.

We hadn't been there, but had heard of them from others and could relay them in small club-like gatherings.

Some adults say they've taken a leap of faith with no assurances and are astounded at the bounty, spiritually, and temporally of the leap.

There's the calling for each one of us—I believe that surely—but we can refuse the call.

Not availing ourselves of the risk, not stepping into the mystery when it's presented, is the grinding down of a counterfeit safety.

A toe in the water is kindergarten, perhaps a start or merely a sop.

What is the world showing you?

Here's What You Owe Others

SHOWING

"Let me show you,"
she said.
It lit me up—
her saying those
words—
and I wonder why.
It wasn't the stuff.
It wasn't the trick.
So I took her lead.
I offered
to show people.

Same thing!

Sometimes I wait when there's
no reason.

Perhaps I'm fearful that I'm really not
good enough to deliver the goods.

But then somebody pushes me or
asks me or even demands that I give
what I have.

So, then I do.

I take my know-how or my
experience or my gift in some way
and lay it on the line.

The results blow them away, the
recipients grateful, and I'm clearly
a contributor.

OK, next time, no hesitation! What
else am I here for?

Tell Me About It

CRAFTSMAN

That thing you do so well—
about which you're silent,
do you take it for granted?
I think not;
were I to ask,
you could speak
at length about it,
how you came
to learn and love it.
Isn't that so?
You're respected,
that's clear, and
people are better off
for your efforts.
So let us rejoice
in the gift.
Come now,
tell me about it.
Still, there
will be secrets
even you don't know.

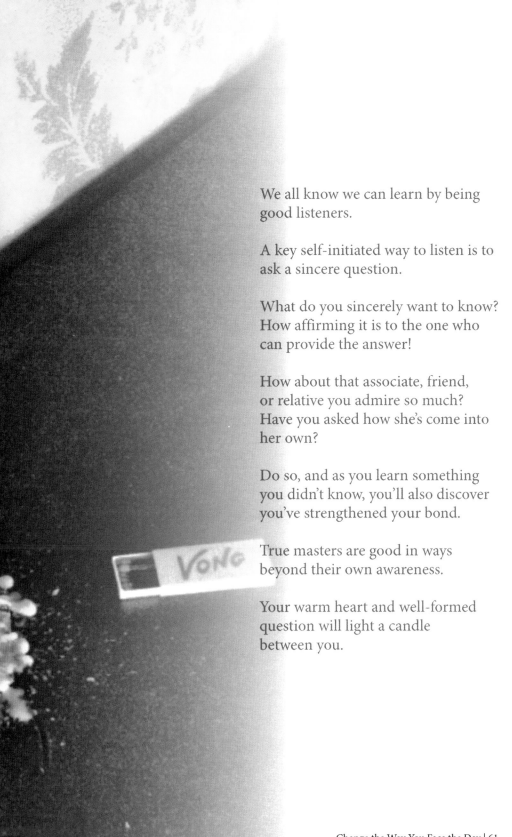

We all know we can learn by being good listeners.

A key self-initiated way to listen is to ask a sincere question.

What do you sincerely want to know? How affirming it is to the one who can provide the answer!

How about that associate, friend, or relative you admire so much? Have you asked how she's come into her own?

Do so, and as you learn something you didn't know, you'll also discover you've strengthened your bond.

True masters are good in ways beyond their own awareness.

Your warm heart and well-formed question will light a candle between you.

Change the Way You Face the Day

A Note from the Author
Questions for Discussion

A Note from the Author

Before you bought you this book, you probably noticed or heard it was set up in an unconventional way. True enough, so let's ask why I would start with poetry if the idea is to get your heads on straight in facing the challenge and opportunities each day lays out in front of us. The answer is simple: in poetry, we have a medium that conveys the maximum amount of information in the smallest amount of space. Think about it, one thing poetry isn't is wordy. And because its meanings are sometimes hidden around the corner, how great is it that we will engage our heads and hearts together to make discoveries that, at times, may blow our minds and deeply affect our lives.

Small groups are resourceful and creative but not always easy. There's a skill or discipline required to get the most out of them. Groups for our purposes should be in the range from 5 to 9 members. Smaller than that they lack diversity and energy; larger, and they fall into a few dominating, vocal people while others withdraw and remain silent. This is not arbitrary as studies support this process.

So here's the main rule: at the beginning of every meeting, the facilitator will ask each member in turn to share his or her reaction, impression, or question about the reading (a chapter or set of chapters) in 30 to 60 seconds. This is done in succession without any comment or question from any other member. After the round is completed, any member can ask any other member for clarification on his or her statement. The group has begun its process and the facilitator can proceed with his or her plan for discussion or launch discussions created by the initial sharing, or the questions posed at each chapters conclusion. Be flexible and spontaneous. Go with the flow. This is best and most fun. This method is most likely to lead to vitality, staying power, and overall success of the effort.

It may well be that the group's success will result in wanting to invite others to join, or others when hearing of the vitality and energy of the group, may ask to join, and all that is simply great! You may want to accommodate this energy. But to do so you have to have volunteers be willing to split and start new groups to maintain the integrity of the 5 to 9 member rule. Ignore this, and you most likely will not succeed.

Questions for Discussion

What Do I Do Now?

1. How do you have feet of clay?

2. What is the significance of the river?

3. What are some means of evaluating old convictions?

4. What subtle ways do you run from your fears rather than face them?

5. When is it wise to put a concern on hold?

See How We Look Up

6. Is there such a thing as secular worship? If so, what is it? Can it be described?

7. Is the furtive bow more felt than seen? Do you have your own way of bowing?

8. Do you have some art in your quiet place? What does the art mean to you?

9. What do you have at your back?

10. Is there an arch or dome important in your life? Would you like to describe it?

Visions in the Backyard

11. Think about your own backyard. What was it like? Perhaps you didn't have a backyard. Did you have a balcony in your apartment building? Did you have something else?

12. What took you outside as a child? How did nature impact you? Did you have a favorite tree?

13. What flower meant most to you? Why?

14. Did you have a teacher in school that made you think about nature?

15. Did you go on picnics?

When Life is Living in the Fold

16. What does the photo say?

17. How does the "Her" in the poem affect you?

18. Is the man a bit of a doter? Is the man a bit too much?

19. Is the love here a bit syrupy?

20. How does love make solitude rich? Does it, really?

Life in Firefly Village

21. Do you ever see fireflies anymore? They seem almost extinct.

22. What neighborhood activity took place spontaneously in your youth? Would it make sense today, where you live? What activity could take its place?

23. OK, dads were central in the example. Where could moms and daughters fit in? What would their activities be like?

24. What does the photo say?

25. What good will are you exercising these days?

That Thing Is Life in the Wings!

26. Has an "It" been looking you back in the mirror?

27. Is "It" just a matter of doing it? Or fixing a plan, then following it through? Or is it something else? Care to share it with others or with this group?

28. Are you eager to show your stuff? That's not necessarily vain is it? Could you say, "I just wondered if I could really do it, and I did!"?

29. What if you don't know how to proceed? Who can you talk to for some good listening on both ends of the discussion?

30. It is okay to admit you're afraid, that you might fail. Would it be a disaster if you did?

The Way It Is

31. OK, you made a mistake. It doesn't have to stay a mistake, does it? Share one example of fixing a mistake that you thought was powerful in its effect.

32. Haven't you made mistakes that later led to you being on a different path that worked out well? Are you willing to tell us about it?

33. What would it be like for you to purposely not be in control of some activity or situation you're engaged in and to just let it happen?

34. Is there a time when you were startled and frightened, yet everything turned out well? If yes, what did you learn?

35. How frequently do you ask others, "What do you think?"

When the Seemingly Insignificant Isn't

36. Do you ever pull photos out of a shoe box or view an album that just fills you with pleasure and memories?

37. What about a trip or a party you planned with a friend that turned out to be an absolute blast and people still talk about it? What made the trip or party so special?

38. Was there a moment in your life in the past week that was really special, but for some reason you dismissed it or let it go by without appreciation?

39. Do you have a must in your life? Is there something you "must" take on, but haven't? Are you willing to acknowledge that it's a life-blood must? Then get at it—Now!

40. Are you willing to ask for help from someone to help you carry the "life-blood must" out? Are you willing to let someone else know you're committed and are going for it?

See What Isn't There, Then Put It There

41. Does fantasy strike you as a waste of time and effort? Does thinking about your grownup version of the big bad wolf who'll blow your house down scare you? Are you not willing to take him or her on or to use your true strength?

42. What does the photo say?

43. Do you remember the book from the 70's, *The Secret of Cat Dancing*? An ordinary housewife in central Indiana with no publishing credits wrote it in her attic and it became a phenomenal best seller. Do you want to look into this great story? Do you think the ordinary housewife could believe it?

44, Think maybe you ought to take a little *time-out* and put your feet up?

45. Your creation, whatever it is, is yours. Perhaps you can look at it in a way that you've never seen? Are you willing to take a good and patient look?

It Comes in on Little Cat Feet

46. What kind of pleasant surprises have you had when someone intervened in your life or work in an unexpected way?

47. How have people so gentle turned out to be effective for you? Have you actually had that experience? If so, how did that gentleness present itself, in what form?

48. When has the charismatic person, who arrived with such fanfare and charm, turned out to be a disappointment? Or has that not been true for you but just the opposite?

49. Who has been a dominant and unforgettable model for you? Did that model appear early in your life or in more recent times? How do you still feel his or her presence?

50. Are you aware of anyone who sees you as his or her model? If yes, how does that make you feel?

Be Present at the Creation

51. In your adulthood, what means do you employ to fill your life with ample, pleasurable options? How do you have a good time?

52. Do you know someone who has won your respect for taking considerable risk in work or personal pursuits and found success you admire? What have you learned about his or her experience? Could it also be true of you?

53. Can you take some practice steps to see how the mantle of achievement, which you admire, feels on your own shoulders? Do you know how to ask for help? Do you know how to get the training and support you need?

54. Do you feel you have a calling?

55. What is your concept of destiny? Do you have one?

Here's What You Owe Others

56. Do you play it safe? Are you courageous enough to know it and therefore see it?

57. Where has playing it safe got you?

58. How can you break the pattern? What are the real answers? What must you do?

59. Have you heard this expression—*What you want wants you*? If you could bring yourself to believe it, how might this statement energize you? If it's true, there's nobody else quite like you on the planet. What's more critical than you finding out what you want?

60. Do you feel you have to be perfect? Do you know you don't have to be perfect? Do you doubt this? Are you willing to ask this question of the people you admire?

Tell Me About It

61. In earlier chapters, have I (the author) not encouraged you to get help from the people you admire?

62. Do you see a strong endorsement of that idea in this chapter?

63. Are you more confident that people you admire are willing to support and offer their advice generously to you?

64. Do you know people who might be willing to share their experience in getting help and counsel that put them on their own growth path?

65. What secrets might you not know?

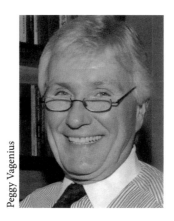

Peggy Vagenius

ALLAN COX is a CEO, author and poet. Founder of Allan Cox & Associates, Inc., he has authored ten previous books. These include the best sellers *Confessions of a Corporate Headhunter* (the first book ever written about the executive search profession), *Inside Corporate America*, *The Making of the Achiever*, and *Straight Talk for Monday Morning*. He has advised CEOs and top management teams of many corporations and not-for-profit organizations, including USG, Motorola, Consolidated Communications, Columbus McKinnon, Kraft, Pillsbury, the Minnesota Vikings, Child Welfare League of America, and *The Christian Century* magazine. He served for five years as chairman of the board of Chicago's Center for Ethics and Corporate Policy. He and his wife, Cher, live and maintain offices in Chicago and San Diego.

6652112R00042

Made in the USA
San Bernardino, CA
12 December 2013